# Growing Through Concrete

## Dandelion's Magnificent Journey

**Also by Jessica Moore**

*DandyLion's Magnificent Journey* – children's book

# Growing Through Concrete

## Dandelion's Magnificent Journey

## Jessica Lynn Moore

*DandyLion Ministries*

First Printing: 2019

ISBN 978-0-359-91352-7

DandyLion Ministries
9301 Hog Eye Rd, #216
Austin, TX 78724

To Mobile Loaves & Fishes

After 15 years on the streets, thank you for giving me a place to call home.


To my Mother Linda

Thank you for giving me life. I thank God every day that you are back in mine.

# Contents

# Foreword

A note from the editor

I first met Jessica in the Fall of 2018 at the Art House at Community First! Village in Austin, Texas. The Village is a remarkable place where the chronically homeless are relocated into micro-homes and are surrounded by a rich community with which to engage. Jessica and her wife Bridgette are two of the 30 artists who live and work at the Village. At the time, I was finishing a master's degree in Media Arts and Worship from Dallas Theological Seminary and working at the Art House for my internship.

November 1st, 2018 was a day I will not soon forget. Jessica and Bridgette were preparing mounds of ornaments to sell at the upcoming Christmas Village of Lights, the music was blaring, and everyone was in a festive mood. Jessica was singing along, and I commented to her that she always seemed to know all the words to whatever was playing on the radio. Jessica said, "No I don't, I can't even remember all the words I've written." I asked what she meant, and she began to recite something very fast. I asked her to slow down, but she couldn't seem to remember it slower. It was then that she got out her iPad and showed me some of her writing. I read the first few paragraphs silently and looked up at her. "Jessica, did you write this yourself?" She nodded yes. I began to read aloud, the room became quieter, people started listening, and Jessica paced back and forth as bits and pieces of her life, her understanding of the world, and her deep faith began to surface. "Jessica, I believe you are a creative writer," I said in a reverent tone. "This is wonderful!" She repeated the words slowly, "Creative writer, I don't know what that means. I've heard my writing called stream-of–consciousness, but..." I explained that it meant she was able to write in creative way, and that I thought it was really good. At this point, she became emotional, and ran from the room. In her absence, Bridgette explained to me that Jessica was severely dyslexic, and that she could barely read or write. It turns out that when she is inspired to write something, she speaks into the microphone on her iPad, using the Voice to Text option, and the words are written out for her.

When she returned, Jessica told me that her poems spontaneously appear in her head, and they stay. I can attest to the fact that she has them memorized down to the last if, and, or but. Yes, they were raw. Yes, the punctuation and spelling often make her meaning unclear, but I began to realize over the next few days what an important work this could be. Here was a glimpse into the life of someone who had been abused, neglected, and chronically homeless. Someone who had begun and completed the odyssey of a sex change, was now married, and living at Community First! Village. I felt her words could offer an important step to understanding the culture and devastation of homelessness. Added to which, I had studied creative writing in seminary, and felt I could possibly help her.

What you are about to read is a mixture of Jessica's autobiography and her poetry, which I have come to call her "proverbs": short pieces of wisdom about the world according to Jessica. The "proverbs," are written with mostly lower case letters, very little punctuation, using only spacing to lead you to her intended meaning. I think you will be very surprised at the approachability of her work. It invites you in, as does she. She has a rhythmical sound to her pieces, which is not surprising given that her influences are Dr. Seuss and Shel Silverstein. While not written in iambic pentameter, her proverbs have that feel.

It also has not been lost on me that without modern technology, this book would have been impossible—her thoughts would have remained hidden in her head. But could it be that God ordained for her to have an iPad at her disposal, living and working at Community First! Village, with an intern who had the time and basic knowledge to help her, all for "such a time as this."

Enjoy,

Janet Mabery Fulmer
Editor

# Introduction

The original manuscript was stolen. I wrote it when I was 18, and I don't think I'll ever be able to rewrite it. The original story was a children's story. I gave up and did not start writing again until February 19th, 2013. I was 34 years old, 16 years after the fact. Bits and pieces from the original manuscript are in the updated version.

To the reader: be mindful! There are a lot of grammatical errors! A lot of run-on sentences with no punctuation. But if you can read and follow along then it shouldn't matter. Thank you...

# New Beginnings

this book is
based on a true story...
but then again
no
not really
some of it is
but the rest
may never be
might as well have never been
yet this is the end

meaning no offense
and hopefully none is taken
but something in my soul is shaken
this is the start
of something new
and it regards you

it's up for you to decide
the fact of the matter is
i no longer need to hide

# Reality

reality is like a collage
or something you can decoupage

it could be a theme to your existence
or a covering of omittance
truth is like a mirage—
you see it
but is it really there?

yes
for some it's a reality
for others only a possibly

my truth may not mirror yours
but there is still a reflection

# I am mentally delayed

I have a LD (learning disability), was BEH (behaviorally emotionally handicapped); I have ADD (attention deficit disorder), and I am mentally delayed. I keep telling people that I can't read and it's not that I can't: the fact of the matter is, it is hard for me to read. I'm not bipolar or schizophrenic though somewhat paranoid. I do have PTSD, and you will find out why. I've been in behavioral, emotionally handicapped classes. I still have not found out whether I'm autistic, but from what I've been told, I'm very intelligent. I've been in and out of psychiatric wards my entire life. I've had a few EEGs done to my head, but nobody can tell me what's wrong with me. Not saying there's anything wrong with me!

# Kaleidoscope

it's just an analogy
on how things could be
not the way they are
it's like looking at a star
from so so far
what you see isn't always what you get

it's like telling a half truth
as opposed to the whole truth
it's like reading a book
without words on the page

i know they say
less is more—more or less
but does anybody know what i'm trying to address?
it's considered a stress factor
like i'm the grass and you're the tractor
pulling up weeds instead of planting seeds

life in all its colors
people and all the mess
often my thoughts and dreams leave a residue
a skewed color trail inside my scrambled-up head
the images spin
twist and turn
and into my memory they do often burn

but how do i sort them out?
is there any pattern in the madness?

any sense to its chaoticness?
sifting through my thoughts
is like rummaging through a junkyard for the items lost
which desperately must be found

God, help me!
my feet aren't on the ground
should i step out onto the water
and take a leap of faith
only Your love can calm me
keep me safe and awake

my thoughts are like a kaleidoscope
they're images that make no sense
and i do not know if they will ever let me rest
i pray for peace
wisdom
and love
that You sweet Lord
will help me see myself more clearly
before this kaleidoscope nightmare
drives me to the edge of insanity

# Random Thoughts

random thoughts are like an infection
but this time i'm going to take them
in a different direction
of not what's just in my head
but of words that have never been said
so come along and gather round
cause what was lost will soon be found

come, come along
gather round—there's no need to clown
we are who we are
so come, sit down
pull a chair up to the table
have a seat
i'll buy you a beer
would you like something to eat?

i am here to enlighten you
not to frighten you
there's no need to fear
there's something i wish to tell you
so come and hear
i'll be sure to make everything crystal clear

i had an idea and
ideally ideas they come + go
thoughts are the same way
but if you don't write them down
they tend to go away

thinking thoughts generally leads
into having good ideas
the gears in my head are turning
everyday i'm learning
creations come from inspirations
but how does a person get inspired to create?
where do the inspirations come from?
or better yet how does one inspire someone else?

what is the whole concept of
"speak when spoken to?"
if nothing is ever said
would nobody ever talk?
think before you speak
your random thoughts!

# Searching

can you help me out?
i'm in a pickle
i'm in a bind
i can't even figure out the thoughts
the feelings
the emotions
running through my mind
i'm looking for something
something i just cannot find
i'm loving
generous
and kind
yes
i'm moving forward
but i'm still just so far behind

questioning always questioning
the tongue is sharper than any two-edged sword
it cuts like a knife
and yet the pen is mightier than the sword
i don't get it
i don't understand
it's a wonderful life
or at least it should be
it's supposed to be grand
will anyone stand with me?
come along and take my hand
i'm on a mission
going to a new land

the past is gone
the future is yet to be seen
where the grass is green
and the air is clean

# I am adopted

I was born November 13th, 1978 in Concord, North Carolina which is in Cabarrus County. I was born on a Monday, November 13th, but every so often it's on a Friday! Hint, hint. From what I was told, I had a perfect birth, but sometime after I was born I lost oxygen to my brain. I was also told that my mother broke my nose. I was 18 months old when I was taken away from my biological mother. Also, from what I was told, my biological dad was summoned to court to claim me, but he never showed, and I became a ward of the state.

I was approximately 3 years and 11 months old when I was adopted. After I was adopted, I was raised in Durham, North Carolina. I've never met my biological family, but the people I grew up with are dead. They are the ones I called mom and dad. Nobody liked my adoptive parents and if you knew my parents, you probably wouldn't like them either. I don't know much about my childhood and even getting into my adulthood, I know very little.

When I was 13, I found out that I was adopted. I was raised as a Carrington, but my adoptive mother told me that my last name was Moore and/or Morgan giving me very little to go by. She also said I have a half-brother name Scott and/or Scottie who is approximately 18 months younger than me. Apparently, we were in the same foster care together, but we were not allowed to be adopted together. We have the same mother but different dads. Other than that, I don't know if I have any other siblings[1].

---

[1] In 2019 Jessica found her birth mother through Facebook. She has since visited her in North Carolina. Jessica found that she has three half-brothers, one half-sister and two stepbrothers.

# Family

Mama moves mountains momentarily
meanwhile maintaining moving morons

Daddy dances around daisies
dutifully denouncing danger

Brother bounces back
bravely beating bullies

Sister simply stands
silently screaming

## Leo the Lion

Leo the Lion was my grandfather
don't laugh!
Jasper Leo Johnson
has always been
and will forever more be
Leo the Lion!
ever since i could remember
from the age of 4 and up

# Bumble Bee

at the age of 4
when i lived at british woods apartments
in durham, north carolina
i saw a lot of kids swatting bees
and it seemed like fun
i swatted a bee
and then i stepped on it
and then i picked it up
long story short
i got stung
the bee stung my pinky finger

# I have a 6<sup>th</sup> grade education

I was taken out of school at the age of 13 so I could take care of my mother. At the time I was told the only reason why I was taken out of school is because the students were a bad influence on me.

My parents were supposed to be homeschooling me. They said that I did not want to learn. The truth is they did not want to teach me. I do remember reading out of one of two books: 2300 English and 2700 English, but I don't know which one. They ended up graduating me at the age of 17, giving me a pissant certificate of completion which means nothing because if I ever wanted to get into the service, that certificate of completion wouldn't amount to a hill of beans. If I was going to do anything it would've had to come from a high school, or I would've had to have a GED.

My adoptive father was always stealing my money. He was stealing my money for years. I got a grant to go back to school when I was 18. That money was to go for paying bills. He took my money, and he smoked it and drank it away and I believe that is what killed him.

So I still don't have a high school diploma, but I'm working on getting my GED.

# Yearning

it's been a year and she is yearning
she is yearning in hopes of learning
the hope
it is burning
a burning flame
driving her insane
she can't figure out what to do
in the midst of the heist
she calls upon the name of Jesus Christ
a thirst for knowledge
a hunger for righteousness
she unclamps her fists
blows a kiss
now school is just about to dismiss
she rolls up her sleeves
walks away
and thanks God for another day

# Just a note

i know how to quote
not so much on how to paraphrase
not much of a synopsis
just a note
a note to one's self
and/or to a loved one

# Where Did the Time Go?

it was 1996
10 o'clock at night
and i'm going to bed—
i blinked my eyes
and it's morning, 6 am

it is said time flies when you're having fun
but a complete 8 hours were missing
where did they go?
i would like to know
because there was no indication
that i had ever been asleep
i don't remember waking up
or counting one single sheep
where did the time go?
for i do not know

# I was abused

Growing up, I was always a fond believer of the Lion, the Lamb, and the Dove. I have a logical explanation, even though you might not think so. I got baptized and accepted Jesus Christ into my life as Lord and Savior at the age of nine. My dad was supposed to be a minister, my adoptive dad, that is. He had a minister's placard hanging on the wall.

Ever since I can remember, my dad would not stop trying to put his hands on me, and/or grab me. He said that it was something my mom's dad and his dad used to do to them all the time. I told him "I don't care what they did to you. I don't like it. Please stop!" He never did. My mom asked me if he had ever raped me, and I told her that I did not know.

At the age of eleven I told him, "If you are not nice to me, my lion friend will eat you up." He looked at me like I was crazy. I told him that my lion friend was standing right behind him, and I could see him as clear as the nose on my face.

He did not stop until I was 28.

# Actions Over Words

my life is in ruins from

*i'm sorry*
*i apologize*
*i will never do it again*

actions speak louder than words
words have no meaning
without the action behind them
people say things
but their actions will prove them a liar
you can tell someone you love them
but yet you're always hurting them
actions over words

*i'm sorry*
*i apologize*
*i will never do it again*

how many times have these words been said
and there were no actions behind them

*i'm sorry*
*i apologize*
*i will never do it again*

actions speak louder than words
so show some actions
and your words will be heard

# Choices

everyone should know
the difference between right and wrong
but this is not about knowledge
because you should already know without knowing

the things that you see
should not be the only reason
you do the things you do
is seeing believing or is believing seeing?
only you can make that choice

every day you make a choice
and the choice should come from one voice

so why do we do the things that we do?
when someone says the devil made me do it
the devil didn't make you do anything
it was your choice
you chose to listen to that voice
but when God speaks you should hear
what he whispers in your ear

# Lion, Lamb, Dove

do you understand the reason why
the lion never ate the lamb
or maimed the dove?
it was all in the name of love

the LION will protect me
the LAMB will take care of me
the DOVE will guide me
they're one in the same
just call on His Name

i turn my allegiance to Jesus Christ
for He is the one who paid the price
my heart is in the right place
but right now i need to keep a steady pace
i know one day i'll be in Your loving grace
standing there with you face to face
walking with you side by side
for in You i will no longer hide
my pain will subside
and You will wipe away every tear that i have cried
thank You!

## Protect Me

dear God
please put a shield of protection around me
in times of turmoil
in times of rage
maybe it was You who set the stage
maybe it wasn't
i'm just asking You to
please
please
turn the page
i'm like a bird
trapped in a cage
i'm here tonight
telling You this isn't right
i'm on the right track
but i need You to have my back

# God Speaks

I SPEAK
i cry every single day
but the reason is unclear
things in my life
are much harder than they appear
for You it may seem easy and nothing to fear
yet i am here!

i'm trying to figure out
how to let You know what i'm all about
You've known me from birth
even before i came to earth
You know my heart
and yet You knew from the start!

i hardly ever pray
but i think of You everyday
i just never know what to say
like someone said in a demonstration
think of it as a conversation
so here I go...

my life is in ruins from
*i'm sorry*
*i apologize*
*i will never do it again*

i can't help myself
i never speak how i feel

but the things that i say are
to my knowledge all real
i don't remember half the things i say
or half the things i do
and yes
the only one who knows me is You


GOD SPEAKS
This may come as some surprise
and to whom it may concern—
I have heard all your cries,
the pain and sorrow.
No need to fear
no worries
I am here.
I am listening everyday
I hear your prayers
I see your tears.
Your heart is pure
and I'll say aloud
"Well done my good and faithful servant,
you have made me proud.
Never stop believing.
Keep the faith."

I SPEAK
i need to be moving forward
but i'm so far behind
i can't even describe what's going through my mind
it's so busy
and it's making me dizzy
my God
i am here
and very much sincere
yet You tell me
there's nothing to fear

GOD SPEAKS
Yes, this much is true
your mind is racing,
and I know what you're facing.
There is nothing to fear,
in time everything will be clear.
Just be still
and know I am here.

# Five People

i had five people living in my head
but to me
they are all dead
not one
not even two
but all five of them
done
finished
finito
through
i'm not the same child you tried to corrupt
i'm a lot stronger than she will ever be
you have no power over me!

# No more

no more i'm sorry
no more excuse
no more bruises
no more abuse

i've had enough
no more clouded memories
no more seeing stars
i'm sick and tired of the many scars
no more scattered thoughts
no more empty promises
no more!

i can promise you this
i've got something you can kiss
get out of my head!
and as far as i'm concerned
you're already dead

no more lies
i can see right through your disguise
surprise
i'm breaking all the ties
look into my eyes
in the end
i will rise!

a new beginning for me
but for you
ho ho
man, you're through!

from this day forward
i will thrive
i will strive
i will survive
no longer will you be a stain on my brain
i'm done with the pain
no longer will i be silent
and no more will i be violent

you've hurt me far too long
and this is me now
i am strong

# I am autistic

I still have not found out whether I'm autistic. I'm just trying to give ya'll a little background information and perhaps it will let you see why I am the way I am.

When I was ten years old, I went to school: Hillandale Elementary, in Durham, North Carolina. My teacher once said, "Did you get up on the wrong side of the bed today? I think you got up on the wrong side of the bed. You need to start getting up on the right side of the bed then you won't be so grumpy." I took her advice literally. As soon as I got out of school, I went home and started pushing my bed up against the wall. My dad walked in on me and asked, "What are you doing?" I said, "My teacher told me to get up on the right side of the bed, so I'm pushing the bed up against the wall so I can." He told me that was just a figure of speech. But at the time, I didn't know what a figure of speech was. I'm stupid, right? No, just misinformed.

# They Say

they say,
3 strikes and you're out
good things come in packages of 3
third time's the charm
though that's not in the Bible

they say,
good things come to those who wait
if at first you don't succeed, try try again
though that's not in the Bible

they say,
God helps those who help themselves
though that's not in the Bible

And, they say,
cleanliness is next to godliness
that too, was never in the Bible

# Broken Mirror

i broke a mirror
i don't believe in bad luck
to tell you the truth
i don't believe in luck at all
i only believe in miracles
that being said
i will not have seven years bad luck
only blessings

# Problematic Overture

this is a problematic overture
in hopes of one day there will be a cure
sure, why not?
so you give it all you got
but still it's a problematic overture

this is a systematic overload
you work so hard
and they just took away your green card
this is taxing i do know
and you feel there's no one you can turn to
nowhere you can go
so it's back to being a problematic overture

this is a systematic overload
you've just lost your way and it's getting dark
you find two roads
so which one to choose
the one to the left
or the one to the right
hurry! hurry!
it's almost night

this is *not* a problematic overture
or a systematic overload
God will make a way where there seems to be no way
He is a candle in the dark
and a guiding light

# Maybe

i didn't do it
don't blame me
it ain't my fault
stop yelling at me!

could it
should it
would it

is it going to be?
i don't know!
kinda,
sorta,
perhaps,
maybe!

# I died twice

When I was 15, I ran away from home. Last thing I remember was leaving Blockbuster Video at 10pm, because they were closing. I started walking home and woke up three days later at the hospital. I had been hit by a car. Apparently, I died twice on the operating table. April 19th, 1994. I remember very little about that day. I don't remember the accident at all. I remember waking up one time and asking where I was. I couldn't see anything and that was the last thing I remember. Eventually when I came to, my girlfriend and her mother were there. I have been alive for over 19 years since the accident, and I am thankful for my life.

## Pearly White Gates

my life
which is no longer in balance
had finally come to a halt
and honestly
it was my fault
it was never about me
well
maybe it was
to a certain degree
why was i so blind?
why couldn't i see?
i don't want to die
living a lie
they told me not to let it go to my head
but i believed everything they said
i was trying to stay strong
but what they were telling me was
so
so
wrong

i'm at a loss for words
a standstill
as i stand here today
trying to pray
i don't know what to say
something's in the middle of the road
blocking my way

my journey began
when i opened the door
but i've been down this road
many times before
at least that's what i thought
i tried to remember
what it was i sought
and i couldn't remember
a single thing that i was taught

confusion was setting in
couldn't remember where i was
i was in such a frenzy
my head all a buzz
my vision was hazy
things were going crazy

i blinked rapidly trying to open my eyes
and who did i see
but the father of lies
i was counting my breath
trying to feel my heartbeat
as i stood there i thought
THIS WILL NOT END IN DEFEAT!

vanity
envy
jealousy
everything that was perplexing to me
all a bunch of lies
and i could see right through his disguise

God help me!
i will win
i will rise

i ask for guidance
and a peace that passes all understanding
i've come to the throne room Almighty God
and with the preparation of the Gospel of Jesus Christ
my feet are shod
i can't do this alone!
give me strength
as i step out and into the unknown

# Still Here

i have been brave
i have had courage
i have been lost
i have had blackouts
i have been dead
but i am still here
why am i still here?

# Life after Death

i'm not here to tell you a lie
reach for your dreams
reach for the sky
we're all going to live
nobody's going to die
it's the God's honest truth
something we should have been told from youth
it's gonna be hard for some of you to receive
most of you won't even believe
but when it's time—
we're all gonna leave

*death* is only a word and some of you will say—
"that's just absurd! it's all in your head!"
but what about the ones who are spiritually dead?

# Blessed

i'm as well as can be expected
any better would be a sin
it could be better
but it could be worse
i am blessed and highly favored

# I wanted to be a girl

When I was nine years old, I told my dad that when I was of age I was going to move out to California to become a girl. I told my parents that when I grew up, I wanted to be like Samantha Stevens from Bewitched, a good witch. I also came up with the whole concept of having a spelling bee to see who can make the best spells, not spell words. I really wanted to be a witch. I started watching things like the Craft, Hocus-Pocus, Warlock. I figured that if I was a witch and I knew how to do spells, I could change myself into girl without having the actual surgery.

When I was ten years old, I started wearing my mother's clothes. At 18 years old, I started going out in public dressed in women's clothes.

# Wrong Form

same shit
different day!
God help me i pray
things are not going well
and as it stands
i'm living in hell!

i hate my face,
and God, i hate the color of my skin
tell me is that a sin?
my body's not the right shape
it's taken the wrong form
i hate the state in which i was born
i've contemplated suicide numerous times
but never brought myself to do it
and each time You brought me through it

the scars in my soul
are just like the hole in my heart
they will never go away
over time it will heal
but the pain is there to stay
why is that?
why must i suffer at the expense of others?
why?
is it God's will?

# Myself

i tried for the longest time to be perfect
then i found out that nobody's perfect

i was always told that
i don't need to be somebody else
i just need to be myself

# I worked at the Waffle House

I started working at the Waffle House on my 18th birthday, which pissed my parents off. According to them, they went to the Waffle House for my birthday, not for me to get a job. BumbleLion was a name I chose for myself when I worked at the Waffle House. I actually had it on my nametag. I worked the night shift and I had to deal with all the drunks, all the people leaving the bars at 2am. I started getting the comments like "faggot, fairy, fruitcake!" And I also got the statement, "I don't want a gay person cooking my food!"

The Waffle House wasn't the only job I had. I worked other places: Orange Enterprises, PTA Pizza, Byrd's, Food Lion, Hardee's and The Durham Exchange Club. But the Waffle House was the longest job that I've ever worked at. I worked there for seven years on and off to be exact. I was there every day, sick or not, and I was told that if I did not come in I would be fired. I was the best damn cook that the

Waffle House ever had and I was even told that. I still had to stop working there at the age of 24 because I became homeless, and they said that I was now unreliable.

# H8

positive actions
will be rewarded with positive reactions
so put all negativity aside

i'm all about love
not hate
so √yourself
@ the door
b4 u enter

# Nobody Understands Me

nobody understands me
nobody hears my pleas for help
my many screams
or if i tell them about my messed up dreams
but that's how it seems
i've been told to shut up
Lord fill my cup
i don't want to stand out
but i do want to stand up

i'm trying to give the best i can
in the words that i say
in the life that i live
i know You can hear me
why is it they jeer at me?
why?
do they fear me?

maybe i've done something wrong
i'm just trying to tell my story and sing my song
i live by the creed
i stand at Your command
fill my cup
take my hand
take me on home to the promised land
GOD help me
help me understand
i'm just trying to follow the footprints in the sand

but my life has been scarred
i have a brand
i had tears of joy
now of sadness
Fuck this shit!
i'm done with the madness
once before
never again
loving someone has become a sin
i give up
now you've done it
you win

# Lock and Key

stress is a mess
God bless me
i had to confess
i hope You don't think of me any less
no more tears
no more fears
but this has been going on for years
i have loved all i could
i've dealt with people's jeers
and constants sneers
but a lot of people
don't use what's between their ears
i'm tired of the hurt
all the pain
sometimes i feel i have nothing more to gain
please forgive me
help me to see
i've given You my heart
lock and key

# Prayer

dear God
help me please
stop the madness
take away the hate
animosity
and discontent
in Jesus name i pray
amen

# Thrive

i'm not pointing a finger
saying no names
but i'm sick and tired of all the games
as we strive to survive
and thrive to stay alive

i'm transitioning
my spirit is not diminishing
i'm living
growing
and yes flourishing
anything's possible
nothing's impossible

# Human

i'm not a presbyterian
pentecostal
mormon
catholic
or jew
i'm a human being
how about you?

nobody understands the true meaning of free
there is freedom of expression
and yes freedom of speech
but who are you to judge me?
who are you to preach?

you don't even know who i am
the words you use don't even reflect who i am
so how many of the lies do you think are true?
i am a human being just like you

# I am transgender

September 13<sup>th</sup>, 2007 when I was 28 years old, in Carrboro, North Carolina, I went to a Hedwig and the Angry Inch concert. At the concert I found out that I was Transgender. That was the start of my transition. I started living my life as Samantha Leigh Carrington.

I don't remember when I started taking hormones, but they had me on Medroxy progesterone and Spironolactone. May 2<sup>nd</sup>, 2008 I left North Carolina and moved to San Francisco, California to finish my transition. When I moved out to California they took me off the progesterone, put me on Estradiol, and kept me with the Spironolactone. I was on injections for a while, but the only way I could get them was from Portland, Oregon.

You have to qualify for transition surgeries because doctors want to make sure you're not going to regret them. I was able to qualify for two surgeries in my transition process because I had already been living as a woman and taking hormones for six years, so they knew I was sure.

I had my orchiectomy back in 2011 on March 13th. I was then put on a wait list for my SRS (sex reassignment surgery), and I was really looking forward to getting it done. It was set for May 6th, 2014. When I first started transitioning, I told everybody that I was going to have my SRS before I was 30, or at least I wanted it done before I was 30. Then I told everybody that I was going to get it before or by the time I was thirty-five. Somebody cancelled, and they bumped me up. On August 27th, 2013, I had my SRS. I was still 34! I guess nothing is impossible if you set your mind to it.

# Unapologetically Me

if i changed would it matter?
all it's going to do is cause a bunch of chatter
if i shaved my mane
i would have to be insane
i'd be taking a ride
a ride on the crazy train
my appearance is mine and mine alone
with all your constant bickering
you think you're grown?

i owed you nothing
it was my pleasure
i gave you what i had
and that's a lot
i'm not my dad
i ain't that bad
i'm a little misunderstood
but i've given you more than i should
but the things that i've given you
i'm glad that i could
if i could bleed for you
don't you think i would?

# Marriage Equality

is this the Obama nation?
if you ask me it's just an abomination
we the People need to be heard
we the People should be heard
each and every one of us have rights
and the system here
it bites
no trans rights
no gay rights
just human rights
a God-given right

trans, bi, gay, straight
we all need to collaborate
there's no need to discriminate
they were right when they came up with
the campaign—no H8
we need to appropriate

if it wasn't for people like them—
there would have never been people like us!
the people with the holier than thou complex
the Bible thumpers
the right wing conservatives

we are the rebels
the heathens
the defiant ones
we are the ones who have been persecuted

we are the ones who are not fit for society
the freaks of nature
the victims of circumstances
it should not be that way!
power is vested unto the people
the ignorant ones—
they are the ones who took our freedom away
slowly but surely it's coming back!
they're on the right track with marriage equality!

# Christianity

christianity is only a religion nowadays
it has nothing to do with spirituality

i hate the fact that
the people who claim to be christians
do not know the first thing about being a christian
i am a christian!
people read the Book
and preach it
but speak out of both sides of their mouth
they tell you
you should love
but they promote hate
they tell you
you should forgive
and accept your fellow brothers and sisters
but they cut you down and slander your name

love thy neighbor as thyself,
do unto others as you would have them do unto you
judge not lest ye be judged
respect begets respect
what you sow is what you reap
and vice versa

i'm not here to judge
that is not my goal
it is not my role in life

happy people should not be made to feel sad
and sad people should be happy

God is the respecter of persons
He doesn't treat us differently
but equally and the same
and one day it will all work out for the better
believe you me
just wait and see

# We all bleed red

come on, have a seat
come, come, please, sit!
i'm going to tell you something
something you won't forget

the lights are off
the candles are lit
the moon is out...
it's been raining – so the ground is wet
i'm trying to set a peaceful environment
inspiration comes from a word and/or a situation
in order to start a movement
it depends on your behavior
in regards to your neighbor

hear me out
listen to this...
i mean we – we are a community
we all lead different lives
come from different backgrounds
comprised of different ethnicities
and different nationalities
we all shed the same tears
we have the same hurt and pain
we all bleed red

our hearts
in some way or another
are all the same

# Wanted & Loved

love knows no boundaries
love sees no color
love sees you and only you
why can't people see that it makes no difference
whether you are black, white, gay, straight, trans
everybody should be loved

love in harmony
people living in unity
the way it was intended to be
makes no difference gender or color
just as long as you know
there is love
one to another

everyone wants
everyone loves
but everybody needs
to be wanted & loved

# I've had many names

I've gone by several different names, but I don't have multiple personalities.

I had my name legally changed January 14th, 2008 to Samantha Leigh Carrington. My name was already Jason Lee, and there's an actress named Jennifer Jason Leigh, so I took her last name and made it my middle name.

March 26th, 2013 in San Francisco, California I legally changed my name once again. I started going by the name Christina Desireé Holt. That is a long story, and it would be too hard for me to explain it. I had to drop the Carrington.

Between 2014 and 2015 while living in Lake Wells, Florida, Syracuse, New York, and Chico California I went by the name Bella Luna Fioré and I became the BeautifulMoonGirl. I was going as Bella while my name was still legally Christina.

I had my name legally changed again September 9th, 2015 in Austin Texas to Jessica Lynn

Moore. The name Jessica Lynn Moore came about because I wanted to go back to my birth name! While living in Syracuse as Bella, I started doing research to find my birth mother whose last name was either Moore or Morgan according to my adoptive mother. When I found out who she was I wanted to change my name back to my birth name: Jason Lee Moore. But I couldn't go back to a male name, so I picked Jessica Lynn and kept the initials JLM.

Even though I don't have multiple personality disorder, I lived with a different personality each time I changed my name: other people have told me so. Each of these names – whether they're a nickname or a legal name – are part of my story and have made me who I am, and my story is playing out well!

# Christina Desireé

i've already said it—
i am DandyLion
i am she and she is me
Christ-like Desired —
Christina Desireé

my name is Christina Desireé
i live in a small place called my head
it needs to be nourished
it needs to be fed
under sheets beneath my bed
trying to figure out what needs to be said

i'm a happy go lucky gal
with no need to say how
but i would like to show you now
there's no need to edit
but you gotta give me credit
to God be the glory

i am with God and
God is with me
He knows i am trans and
He still loves me

# Queen Lioness

i am the Queen Lioness
there's no need to be formal
you don't have to call me your highness
that's a plus not a minus
the good thing about it is
i don't have to deal with shyness

welcome to my humble abode
pull up a chair, have a seat
who wants something to eat?
whatever it is
you're in for a treat
i hope you enjoy the meal
everything's free
what a deal
and at the prices —
it was kind of a steal
what's mine is yours
but remember
keep the food off the floor
if you follow the rules
there will be more
i'm sorry i have to leave now
but i'll be back
just going to the store

i'm graciously inviting you to join me
in a long drawn out—
oh no wait

this is not a parody
just a party
i'm about to take you into a thought
a thought about prosperity
i hope you know what this means
i'm not trying to spill the beans
but i'm treating you all like kings and queens

all jokers aside
no longer will you feel the need to hide
everyone of you is an ace
and you're welcomed at my place
now wipe those tears away from your face
i'm sorry i have no money for satin and lace
no fight to the finish
this is not a race

it will be a Happy You Year in the New Year
get ready to parade and cheer
if you have no idea what i'm getting at
wait and see
it'll all be clear
once you figure it out
you can have a Happy You Year with me

# I was homeless

I've been homeless on and off since I was 24. I've lived in Oakland, Los Angeles, Santa Maria, San Francisco, and Chico, California. I've lived in Winterhaven, Lake Wells, and Lakeland, Florida. And I've lived in Louisville, Kentucky and Syracuse, New York. I never stayed anywhere longer than seven months. San Francisco was an exception, I stayed there on and off for five and a half years. People were always telling me that I needed to find somewhere and settle down.

# Outcast

what's in my head
is easier done and rarely said
but now it is time for me to speak out
and let you know what i'm all about

i don't mean to seem critical
but i think it's kind of pitiful
being left out or caught in the middle

life is a test
so you give it your best
what of the others—
the homeless
the outcasts
will they ever rest?
will they ever sleep?
i should say the least
when they're running from the beast

hatred is not becoming of you
but what do you do?
you nonchalantly say hi
as you walk on by
i'm thinking
what would Jesus do?
wouldn't He stop and talk with them?
wouldn't He stop and talk with you?

# The Homeless Messiah

i feel a lot better now
my spirits have been lifted
God has just answered my prayers
Jesus Christ even walked around on the streets
and lived on the streets
Jesus Christ didn't have a GED
or a high school degree
why should i think i'm any better?

# I went to jail

I was arrested when I was 26 and then again just after I turned 27. I was also arrested when I was 36 and then again when I was 37.

When I was in jail, I read the Bible and I played War – the card game – with God. Nobody understands me, and I mean nobody! They told me "You can't play War with God," but I did!

In jail I prayed and I prayed and I prayed and I felt like I was getting nowhere with praying. I even yelled at God for not answering me. But He was answering me, I just wasn't listening. I've been out of jail for over two years, and I don't plan on going back.

## Stuck

i'm caught between a rock and a hard place
i'm straddling the fence
i'm trying to make sense
with everything that's been going on
i'm hella tense
i don't know if i can take it anymore
i've done a lot
and it's becoming a chore…
i don't know what to do
so i'm calling up to You

# Alive

sometimes i feel that
i would have been better off dead
and i've even told myself
it would have been better
if i had never been born
but that was a lie
i love being alive
and there's no better feeling

# War with God

prayers are answered
maybe not in a timely manner
but when God deems them to be

in jail i played
war with God
and God let me win
i was playing
war with God
but i was not listening
to what He had to say
He was talking to me
but i wasn't listening
now i am
i have been told by God
and this is the God's honest truth
that i would be persecuted
for being me

# Still Voice

thank you God
for teaching me how to listen
to Your still voice
patience is a virtue
something i've come to realize
and silence is golden

be quick to hear
and slow to speak
but i'm constantly rambling
i've never shut up long enough
to listen
to that calm still voice
inside my head
but there was so much going on!
in some cases
there still is

i've asked You numerous times
to fill my cup
You've never once told me
to shut up
and every time i've prayed
i am thankful that my prayers were delayed

# I am a Christian

I do however know that had it not been for God, I would not be here to tell my story. I was baptized at the age of nine and accepted Jesus Christ into my life as Lord and Savior. I re-dedicated myself five other times over the years. I was raised as a Baptist, and the rest of my life non-denominational. Today I consider myself a "Christian *Guidist*."

I came up with *Guidism* back in 2008, but I can't remember if it was before or after I turned 30, and I can't remember if I was in North Carolina or San Francisco. I do, however, remember being on a bus, and it popped into my head. I remember thinking to myself, "Am I a *Guidist?*" and that was that.

I came up with the whole concept of *Guidism* and how I could be a *Guidist*. In my mind it has nothing to do with religion but instead with spirituality, wherein the Holy Spirit guides you. I believe in the Tri-Unity of God, the three in one: God the Father plans, God the Son perfects, God the Spirit performs.

I'm not trying to deter people from Christianity. That's not what I'm trying to do at all. I'm trying to figure out whether or not I've come up with a new belief.

# Testimony

my love will never surpass the love of GOD's
for GOD is love
for the whole of humanity—
GOD'S NOT DEAD
i for one have a testimony to share
i have done it more than once
and in more ways than one
i have died
and yet i'm still alive
i believe in second chances
and i believe in GOD
GOD has given me another opportunity
and this time— I WILL NOT FAIL!
i will continue to give my life to Him
until he takes me home
call me anything you want to
you will not sway my decision

# New Birth

i have been born
i have been born again
i have been reborn
now i'm thinking of my New Birth
God has shown me the way
and why i need to pray

my New Birth and my growth as a Christian
i have come a long way
to get to where i am today

i would like to talk on New Birth
i would like to write a picture of heaven

New Birth comes after Rebirth
when you take a stand
and fight for what you believe in
in the end you will win
but where does it begin?

when you were born
you either were born the way you were supposed to be
or someone else made that decision for you
it was never really up to you
you can either say you are a boy and/or a girl
but if you did
you were in the wrong for thinking so

i stood up for what i believe in
now it is your time to shine
New Birth is a state of mind
where everything you're looking for was found
and the life you led will cease to exist

in the Bible God said,
"I will create new heavens and a new earth"
I will give you a new body and a new name
for the old one will pass away
you'll have riches beyond your wildest dreams
and you will be happy

# Earth

from the time of birth
the first day we occupy earth—
a world filled with myth and mirth
we are here to conquer fear
to fill this land with love
happiness
laughter
and cheer

praises be to God
the One who gave us life
we should be honored
to be called His wife

when we die
where will we live?
heaven or hell?
God has promised a new life for us
new heavens
and a new earth
filled with riches beyond compare
and a kingdom in which we are the heirs to the throne
there will be no more pain
and nothing more to gain
we will have everything
we've ever needed
now, why is it that we had to occupy earth?

# Planting Seeds

just like the dandelion is a flower
the moon continues to shine
the wind contributes to planting the seeds
as does God
in the same way

God is the wind
and we are the seeds He plants
as Jesus Christ is the living water
the Word of God is our food

# I am a spiritual person

What do you think when you think about spirituality? People think they know the answer. People associate spirituality with religion: religion is man-made, spirituality is not.

Have you ever been sitting at home when all of the sudden you are attacked by nothing at all? I have. My mom always said I had a strong connection to the spiritual realm: I've seen a lot of things and heard a lot of things over the years throughout my life. Some good things, some bad things. Believe me: I am not making this up!

If I were schizophrenic there would be a logical explanation for seeing and hearing things that aren't there. But I'm not schizophrenic.

# Spirituality

blessed be!
come
come along
come with me
i'm gonna take you on a journey
a journey through spirituality

religion is out
spirituality is in
come along with me
and let your spiritual journey begin
*Guidism* is a belief
it is mine to say the least
come and let your spirit feast

# Love your neighbor

over the years religion has gotten in the way
they all talk about love
and how love conquers hate
yet there are so many wars
so many people getting killed
where is the love all these religions talk about?

people are on the defensive
always fighting
not coming together
more like dividing

communication is key
if everybody kept things to themselves
everyone's life would be a mystery
what do they think
they're going to Hell if they tell?
they are like a nut in a shell!

# Holy War

my job here is done
even though i lost
i still won
i am here and you are there
i would like to extend you a little prayer—

my God i am sorry for what i've done
and in the name of your Son!
it was not my right
i had no need to fight
it was everything i sought
but Your war to be fought

# Going Up

it's "what's up?"
not "what's going down?"
you got to look towards the sky
not what's beneath the ground

if you're going to heaven
Jesus Christ is the only way
if you're messing with the devil
you're on the hell highway

in this people don't see the same
and when you talk about God and/or Satan
people say they are lame
we all have religion to blame

if you have an ear to hear
listen…
get out of your head
tell me what was said
the Word of God is your food
and Jesus Christ your bread

# I want to be understood

I don't show emotion well, but I do try to be sympathetic or whatever the word is. Maybe empathy? I don't know: I just want to be understood. If you ask me, my comprehension level is off. I can understand some things, but a lot of things, not so much. You have to keep explaining it to me, and I also get tired of people getting mad at me when I asked them to repeat or explain themselves.

One thing's for certain, I hate having to explain myself. I try to do it without crying. Sometimes I get mad, but it's not because you are asking me the question. It's me trying to explain information that I do not have.

## Open Book

i am an open book
so read my pages
this could go on for ages

my dad was a whore
my mom pretty much a bore
and people always assumed i was rotten at the core
but that was just a lore

i'm an open book
come and see
take a look
nothing fancy
but there's more to me
so come and read—
let me catch you up to speed

i can't help myself
i never speak how i feel
but the things that i say are to my knowledge all real

i don't steal
i never kill
i live for love not war
i just can't stand the gore

i am an open book
so read my pages
i just want to be understood

106

# Speak

think!
ruminate!
my cup is overflowing
there's a lot on my plate
not only do i tend to overthink
but a lot of things seem to gravitate
a gravitational pull
into the rural
if i could only elaborate
i can't concentrate!

i say nothing
just to hear myself speak!
i speak
so that everyone can hear what i've got to say
is it my fault that nobody wants to listen?

what's wrong with a quote
or a motivational speech?
what say you when you hear someone preach?
it's a powerful message
what about the many people they reach?
some will receive it
others may not
but for some of us
it's all we got...

# Known

i found the rhythm in You
which at times is hard to do
create in me a clean heart
for You know it's falling apart

i wish to walk with You
talk with You
but it's hard to find the words to say
it is said we need to pray
and yes everyday
but it's hard to tell You
something You already know

You've known me from birth
You've helped me to grow
what am i to do
where am i to go?

God the father
maker of heaven and earth
You know my heart's desires
and yes
my soul it tires
my voice is being silenced
but i'm not here to show defiance
i wish to be a part
a part of Your mighty alliance

You are the one who is high and lifted up
how many times do i have to ask You to fill my cup?
patience is a virtue
silence is golden
but all this pain
it is not good if i just hold it in
You have told in Your Word
it is good to be heard

# I am often lonely

I have a lot of problems, but then again, who doesn't? I do, however, like talking with people. But unfortunately, I can't bring myself to introduce myself to anybody. I have a lot of things to talk about. I'm not a bad person, but it always seems like people are looking down on me. Then again, I'm a very shy individual, a very unique person. I feel that nobody understands me.

I was told that when I introduce myself, I'm not to talk about myself. I'm supposed to talk about the other person. Let them know that I'm interested in knowing about them, but if you ask me, that sounds creepy. The person might think I'm a stalker, which I'm not. I would, however, like to be more open with people. Meet new faces, sit down, have coffee, lunch, whatever, makes no never mind to me. Just as long as I have someone to talk with, and/or to.

I didn't really have any friends growing up, but the ones that I did have I lost because of the people I called my parents. They say the more friends you have, the lonelier you feel. I don't know how true that is, but the truest of true friends should not make you feel lonely. They should be there when you need them. And as for the ones that leave you, I don't know what to say about that. I can't fathom why a friend would leave another friend.

# True Friend

what is a friend
if not someone you can talk to
or confide in
people say you can always trust your friends
and others say friends are nothing but trouble
they will only let you down
you're better off on your own

good friends
best friends
soul-mates
and then
no longer are they a part of your life
they just cut the ties that bind

friends are there through thick and thin
they're there for the good
the bad
they are there to pick you up
when you're sad
for the true-blue friends that i have
i am glad

# Alone

join me in a conversation
and with me you will see
there is more to me than what you don't

i don't comment on a lot of social media posts
some of them i do
but not the most

i don't read the paper or watch the news
join me in a conversation
but only if you choose

i'm very intelligent
not to boast
join me in a conversation
get inside my head
count the number of tears that i have shed
do you know how many times that
i have wished i was dead?

God take me home
take me on home
for i'm so alone

# In Your Hands

the Lord is my rock
my salvation
on Him i do stand
God
here i am
i'm extending my hand

my life is in Your hands
but i'm caught somewhere in the expanse
between time and space
with a blank expression on my face
i have no thoughts of my own
i'm out here and all alone

i'm trying to take the path that no one will travel
i'm walking upon hard gravel
to be in Your presence
would be so sweet
but these rocks
they're hurting my feet
why should my soul tire?
i'm looking for that spark
that fire

my life is in Your hands God
it's Your will be done
not my own

# I am a writer

I started writing February 19th, 2013 when I was 34. Growing up, I got into authors such as Dr. Seuss and Shel Silverstein which is one of the reasons everything I say comes out as a rhyme, and now my brain works like a human dictionary. Having a learning disability and being four years mentally delayed meant it was hard for me to fit in! So it is hard for me to explain things without rhyming. But if you ask me, I think I'm doing a pretty good job.

# Writing

take out of it what you will
but writing gives me a thrill
i come up with something new each and every day
there's so much more i could say
they say wisdom comes with age
yet writing things down helps me deal with rage
i have anger issues
though not something i would choose
i could never hurt
another living soul
so i'm on a mission
i have a goal

# Leader

i have helped people to the best of my abilities
only being one person
but it has been said
one person can make a difference

i have been told i have a strong voice
though my voice is loud
i don't think that's what is meant

my mom always told me that i could be a leader
though i never thought that could be possible
until now

# Clouds

everything i say is direct
and straight to the point
it just comes to me so i write it down
i'm not insane
i'm not a dunce
i'm not a clown
i hate to be rude
but i don't like kidding around
yes my head is in the clouds
but my feet are on the ground

# Timing

i have a knack
a gift for rhyming
it's like looking for a needle in a haystack
it's all in the timing

# I am honest

I think a lot of things can be put into perspective. I would like to be honest with people instead of dishonest. I like to trust people, but I would also like to be trustworthy. I think honesty and trustworthiness says a lot about a person's character.

# Trust

trust is not given freely
it's something that is earned
i've been told a lot
i'm willing to learn

i trust more than i should
but then again
i try to see the good in people
it's not right being hateful
and nobody should be
it is said
you can't trust everybody
and i agree

it is also said
be mindful of the company you keep
i've heard about the devil in disguise
and a wolf in sheep's clothing
and people who speak with silver-tongues
they speak with deceit
sly and cunning

people think of me as gullible
they take my kindness for weakness
nobody understands me
or why i do the things i do
and sometimes
neither do i
i'm not a bad person

life is confusing
people say
"what is there to comprehend?"
am i that naive to be taken for granted?
is my living in vain?

why must people downplay my intelligence?
it's all good
i'm a lot smarter than people give me credit for

# Rumor has it

it's not all rainbows and butterflies
it's hard to speak the truth when there are so many lies!
some things are better left unsaid
teetering on rumors
which leads into gossip
and everybody's worried about who said or did what
or maybe not
but you didn't get it from the horse's mouth!

telling lies
prevents the truth
from being heard
what is a good lie?
what they don't know won't hurt them
or is it truth hurts?
if you're telling a story
and you leave certain parts out
is that not telling the whole truth?
if somebody is making up a story
off the top of their head
and somebody else knows the real story
what is that considered?

you try to confront that person and they say
"i'm just speaking my truth"
what is that?

# Explosion of Truths

this is an explosion of truths
you will know the truth
and the truth will set you free
there is a truth in everything you
see
hear
and do
even in a lie there is some truth
truth hurts
but should it?

# I am married

I am Transgender. My wife is Cisgender/Bio-Female. I met my wife on Facebook in 2015. I was living in Chico, California at the time.

We were never supposed to be getting married though. Her birthday is October 2nd, so I came down to Texas for her birthday a month ahead of time. I asked her, "What would you say if I asked you to marry me?" She said, "If you're for real, yes, yes, absolutely yes! But if you're just bullshitting me, the answer is no, because I don't want you to get my hopes up for nothing." I bought her a marriage certificate for her birthday, and three days later – on October 5th, 2015 – we got married. People were supposed to come to the wedding, but they didn't. It was just Bridgette, me, and the Justice of the Peace.

Though it has been trying, I do love my wife.

# Stay

i'm insane
trying to maintain
kind of scatter brained
and all my energy has been drained
why am i here?
how did i get here?
where did i come from?
where was i going?
all this indecision
no way of knowing

Why?

i'm thinking too hard
and yes my heart has been scarred
sometimes i think love
has been barred
banned
yet i don't understand
all the tension
i have no comprehension

Why?

how many days must we do this?

Stay!

how many times must i say it?
please don't go away…

there may be times we do not agree
but just hear me out
this is my plea
my love is given willingly and free
please don't take yours away from me

your love is like a tie dye
an explosion of color
a rainbow in the sky
your love is like the fireworks
on the 4th of July

as each day goes by
i think of you
i want to make you happy
please don't cry
i love you
and i will to the day i die

# In the name of love

there is a song you can sing
to let someone know the love you bring
come summer autumn winter or spring

it's never easy to express one's feelings
but if it comes from the heart
that is a very good start

yes actions speak louder than words
and it begins with the first impression
how you present yourself
then again you can't always judge a book by its cover

beauty is on the inside
or in the eye of the beholder
not just skin deep

i know it is said that opposites attract
but i do not believe that is a fact
it should not matter if you are opposite
or the same
when two people get married
it is to become one in union with each other
like two halves make one whole

is it love that makes people do stupid things?
or do people do stupid things in the name of love?
i need some clarity

# Heaven

i'm going home
and you're coming with me!
i put my foot down!
i'm taking you to Heaven!
cause Hell's no place to be!
we're gonna be together
for all eternity!

# Forever and 10 Days

always and forever
forever and 10 days
the days may be hot
some even cold
we will remain young
with no fear of getting old
i've told you once
i'll tell you again
the things we will do
ho ho
if you only knew
come along and take my hand
a walk along the beach
a walk through the sand
when we get to where we are going
it will be grand
a land of fortune
no need for fame
a place of wealth
and everyone knows your name

forever and 10 days.
that's forever tenfold
i'm ready to take the stand
i'm ready to be bold
we're heading for a land
where we're worth much more than gold
take your time
endure the climb

steady your pace
this is not a race
they already know your face

you will always be a part of my life
whether or not you are in my life
you will always be a part of my family
because you are the only family i know
you have joined me
alongside me
in my journey
you were there with me when i laughed
and when i cried
even though i am here
i will always be by your side
for forever and 10 days

# Love of my Life

you do everything you have to
just to hide the hurt
and you try to mask the pain
and you think to yourself
the sun can't shine through the rain
they tell you to take it with a grain of salt
but on the other hand
there's nobody there who will understand

you scream and you shout
but sometimes i think
you don't wanna work things out

by the morning dew
you will hear me whisper
i love you
you're doing your best
at least you are tryin'
now, now, there's no need to be cryin'
i am here
i'm your DandyLion
fly away with me
this world is a mess
i want to get you out of here
and away from the stress
i am your beautiful
sexy
gorgeous
lioness

i'm here to take care of you
this much is true
i'm here to love you
now why so blue?
away from the madness
there's no need for sadness
don't worry
i got this
there is happiness and sweet bliss
now, give me a kiss

how do i love you?
i could count the ways!
i really do love you
i hope you stay
i look at all the strays
but you're the one
you're the one who catches my gaze!
i've asked you to marry me
you said yes
my life is been torn from the past until now
i look at you and all i can say is wow!
you're like a star which has taken flight
look at you
you're out of sight!
soon you will see
and hopefully you'll agree
you mean so much more to me

# I have no children

My children, had I any, would be named the following; Djinn Zoriel (*jin/gin*), Nyasia Koraline (*ni-ay-jah*), Christopher Aiden and Oona Dejahy.

They never came into fruition. They were never born! I myself, cannot get pregnant. I can't give birth! I have no female organs.

I thought that if I had children, I would never treat them the way my parents treated me. I would treat them better than the way I was treated. The way I grew up was no picnic. All of my children would have been taught in the way of the Lord, and they would also have an education. And a childhood, something that was taken from me.

# Trapped

one morning when i woke up
i got trapped in my bed sheets
i was screaming for help
my dad never came
i ended up getting out all by myself
and then my dad showed up

# Phishing Scheme!

2014, when i was living
in winter haven, florida
i got a phone call from a california area code
claiming to be florida social security department
and they told me that i had a $27,000 lien
on my name
come to find out
it was just a phishing scheme!

# I want to write music

I write lyrics, but I'm not too keen on how to add the music to the songs. I was told that I am tone deaf. I know how to play a few keys on the piano, but that's it, and they're not even the right keys. They are the first few keys in: "Joy to the world, the Lord has come. Let earth, receive, her king!"

At the age of 15 I got into Prince. The first song I ever heard was "The Most Beautiful Girl in the World". I even tried to fashion myself after Prince and Rupaul. At the age of 17 my dad told me that I reminded him of Boy George.

# Performance

drop the mic
to do something you like
pick it up
for something new

i can't dance
but i can sing
i'm anything other than average
i just don't wear all that bling bling

when i was a child
i was in children's choir
i love to sing*
a lot of people tell me i have a beautiful voice
and others say
"don't quit your day job"

# Pot of Gold

there are two clouds
one on each side
with a rainbow in the middle
but there's no pot of gold
in this riddle

# Let's Start a Band

you know something?
you wanna get back into music?
i want to sing
we can do this
if we work together

as it is, i am DandyLion.
what would your name be?
the group could be called Trans4mations
we could work together to write the lyrics
this is a transitional period for us both

i am BeautifulMoonGirl
what kind of music would we play/perform?
probably rock
i have so many ideas
we can incorporate poetry
you know how i am with rap + rhyme
but then again
i will need your input as well

what do you think?
i would like your opinion

# Singing Songs

singing songs to one's self
or out in a crowd
some may be mellow
others may be loud
the songs may be off
and somewhat out of key
but what should it matter to you?
it's what makes me happy
just listen to the melody
they may be short
some even long
just listen
there's a message in the song
singing songs simply to say
are sweet symphonies
of love, loss and longing
or to give someone strength in serious situations
soulful in sounding
soothing the spirit

# I want to start a ministry

I've been trying for the last five years to get my ministry, DandyLion's Ministries a.k.a. the DandyLion Garden, off the ground. As I've grown in my spirituality as a Christian *Guidist*, one thing I've come to realize is that how someone looks on the outside isn't what's important: it's what's on the inside that counts. In my 40 years on this planet, I've realized that a lot of things that were not in my own control have made me who I am as a person. It is rumored that I hate people, and I'm the one who started that rumor. I don't hate people. I dislike people. I hate crowds and drama. Though my life has been nothing but drama.

I would like to start a couple of movements. I am only here to help. It would help everybody out in the long run. The question is, how do I go about starting these movements? The more the merrier, I always say. If anybody should need help, all they need do is ask. As it is, I am homeless and broke. I am an LGBT activist, and I support Autism. Now, hear me out. I support everyone in the Human Race and I also support the Animal Kingdom. I've already adopted the concept, now all I need to do is carry it out. Now if anybody can help me out, and tell me how to do it, I'm all ears.

## Helping Others

i have been thinking
and i have come to realize
i have a need to help others
and i will
in time

i want you all to know
though i haven't much myself
i don't need anything more

money is important
but life is more precious
than to be left without

schooling for those who need it, no-charge
housing, food, and whatever else
i will not be running a shelter and/or a halfway house
i don't care if you smoke or drink
but i would have you be mindful of those who don't
i won't be able to do much, i am on disability
i won't give up!!!

## Someone Cares

America used to be land of the free
home of the brave
you will now be part of land of the brave
home of the free
i guarantee
believe you me
come and see and you will agree
alone, you are now
but here you'll be like, wow!!!
you'll be like
how can this be
someone out there must really care about me
well, i am she

# Refuge

the DandyLion's Free Zone is a welcoming refuge
a treasure trove of opportunities
endless possibilities
anything your heart's desire
let me take you higher
anything you can imagine
no need for a djinn
for a wish on a dandelion
all your troubles will end
this message i send
because i am a friend
and a helping hand i will lend

# End of the Rainbow

your pain is now mine
don't worry everything will be fine
i will go with you
all the way to the finish line

i'm on my way
to the end of the rainbow
once i find out how to get there
and where to go
where reality ends
and dreams begin
can you believe i'm doing it again?
leaving the old
starting anew
living the life
just me and you

on that day
you will know what it was all about
you can reminisce
you should think good thoughts
and weed out the bad ones
only you know what day that is
that being said
you will never know how good you have it
until that day comes

# The Gathering

i have a lot of hopes
dreams
aspirations
i'm heading for my destination
to the whole of creation
to everyone
in every nation
i've started my preparation
my heart will continue to sing
join me
join the gathering

# I am home

I think I have finally found my home in Austin, Texas! In 2010 I was living in Los Angeles which is when I started thinking about Austin. I was in the dentist office and I had gone to get my partials replaced because I previously threw them away by mistake. This dentist office had TVs with different informational slides, and on one TV screen there was a Q&A. One of the questions was "Where is a good place to retire?" Not knowing the answer, I spouted out "Austin Texas!"

I have been living in Austin, Texas, since September 1st, 2015. It is now 2018, September 21st! Exactly three years and 20 days, but who's counting?

My home is at Community First! Village. Community First! Village is a tiny house community for people like us: people who have been homeless. Bridgette was on the waiting list for Community First! Village a lot longer than me, but shortly after we got married, I got put on the waiting list as well. Bridgette and I both had to wait two additional years to move in because they didn't have the trailer ready. We moved to Community First! Village June 8, 2017. I finally have a home.

# Live in the Light

life is too short
in some cases just a taste
it could pass you by
so don't let it go to waste

life is a blast yet—
you're living in the past
the clock is ticking
don't go too fast
live in the present
live for the future

a thought
a memory
everything you sought
they will remain the same
but if you keep living there
you will only have yourself to blame

it is said you can't have light without dark
but if you live in the light
there will be no need for dark
and my motto is live for love
cause love lives in you

# The Garden

come to the garden and grow
you will see there is a radiance
there's a glow
there are many places you can go
breathe the fresh air
take it slow
you can watch the children play
even if you wanted to
you could just pray
and thank God for a beautiful day
and finally at last
just be
and know you are free
don't just take it from me
come and see

the clock is ticking
the cock is crowing
the wind is lightly blowing
the sun is shining
the trees are pining
this is a peaceful and happy place
filled with love and grace
where there's a smile on every face
the gentle breeze
the calm seas
the bees are buzzing
the birds are flying
and not a single soul is crying

no one is fighting
the people are very inviting
so exciting
this is not just a home for the homeless
or a refuge for the refugee
come
come
and claim sanctuary

# I am a dandelion

Throughout history people have attempted to exterminate the seeds of the dandelion flower, but its vitality has resilience beyond compare. As with dandelions, there are those who have no other choice but to live a life of vagrancy, drugs, prostitution, and other crimes associated with homelessness. People have tried to ostracize the homeless, deeming them as weeds in society with no value who only choke-up our social justice system.

I've been told my entire life that I was dumb, stupid, retarded, rejected, no good, I would never amount to anything, and no one will ever love me. But I keep moving forward. I'm not going to let that stop me. At least I'm trying. I am not a weed. I am a flower. I am a dandelion.

# Flower

tattered
torn
ripped
stripped of everything
and still we maintain
it takes us just about everything we have
not to go insane
we have one mind
one brain
some of the time we're happy
but most of the time we're in pain
our body here is only a vessel
and blood courses through each and every vein
we are not a weed but a flower
searching for a higher power

# Risen

heal my heart
cleanse my soul
give me life
make me whole
sovereign Lord
You've cut the umbilical cord
You gave us freedom of will
but we need You
we need You still
we need You to show us the way
we need You each and every day
some people say
"why bother?"
You're our Heavenly Host
Abba, Father
we need nourishment
like a child in the mother's womb
we need You
like a bride needs a groom
we need You and all You come to give
You died so that we can live

# God's Grace

under the Lamb
i know who i am!
i've been colored in faith
just look at my face
we may not be in the same place
but we are all covered by God's grace

## Longing for Love

my heart is amazing
just one-of-a-kind
there's not another like it
not one you can find
living life
longing for love or to be loved
literally losing everything
yet still keeping my faith
seeking serenity in solitude
stepping out of the shadows and into the sun
frail furnishings
in search of fellowship
finding favor
and trying not to fall far from Grace
a lot of things happen for a reason
you'll find the reason
and you'll know why some things happen
God works in mysterious ways
and miracles they do happen
live like you'll never die
but die to live
this is a journey
not into the past
but stepping stones into the future

# Dandelion

roses are red
violets are blue
make a wish on a dandelion
and see if it comes true

i am a vagabond
a free bird
i live off the land
i go where the Spirit leads me
i am a dandelion

a rose
by any other name
would smell as sweet
but a dandelion
will grow up from the concrete

i am a dandelion

# Prequel

i told you my past and my present to be
but a lot of my life is still a mystery to me
i haven't found it's equal
but it's time for me to discover my prequel